" Thinking Aloud "

Published under licence by Brown Dog Books and The Self-Publishing Partnership Ltd, 10b Greenway Farm, Bath Rd, Wick, nr. Bath BS30 5RL

www.selfpublishingpartnership.co.uk

ISBN printed book: 978-1-83952-411-0
ISBN e-book: 978-1-83952-412-7

Cover design by Andrew Prescott
Internal design by Andrew Easton

Printed and bound in the UK

This book is printed on FSC certified paper

MIX
Paper from responsible sources
FSC® C013604
FSC www.fsc.org

"Thinking Aloud"

Chris Callow

BROWN
DOG
BOOKS

Chris Callow Profile

The start of writing poetry was on holiday in St Kitts when I was asked to put an entry in the visitors book. The holiday had been amazing but looking through the previous entries the comments did not seem to say enough so I thought I would write a thank you poem about the holiday and experience. I actually surprised myself and that started the mood of writing, when I got home I jotted down poems about family and friends.

Having had a very varied career and good share of travelling my life has been full of things I have wanted to achieve, rather a transient path with shares of ups and downs, illness and deaths of family and friends.

Now at mid-life, reflection and thoughts play a larger part in my life and it is the writing them down on paper that makes me fathom how to explain these thoughts to myself and to others.

Writing moods can be triggered off by the smallest of things or events, long- or short-lived bouts of time but always good when pen meets paper, yes the pen and paper are first, the computer last.

St Kitts

I went to St Kitts after hurricane George
a tropical island with sun, sea and sand to engorge
The island was damaged to a fair extent
but the locals get on with it they do not relent
The plant life was hit left barren and bare
only nature recovers as if not with a care

I cannot explain the feeling you get
to totally unwind and watch the sun set
The beaches, the sea and all the beach bars
sat there on the sand just under the stars

There only a week was not nearly enough
not going at all would have been far more tough
I must thank my cousin for the accommodation and chance
to make looking at brochures a reality not a glance
I came back to England with a wonderful tan
and can only reflect how lucky I am

The Visitors Book
St Kitts

This place is much more than nice
it is an island paradise
A place in the world that is great to find
so beautifully relaxed and easy to unwind

To arrive and stay in this perfect heaven
my only regrets are that my days here are only seven
Going back home with memories to retain
to last for a while until I come back again

A Positive Need

When I get weary day after day
A voice in my head starts beginning to say
Why do I do it and what will it achieve
There are parts in my life I would love to retrieve
To go back in time is an impossible chore
The problem is now right here at the door

Assess what you have got and where to go next
Disband with the things that get you all vexed
There is always a light that you may not have seen
Decipher the nightmare that is blocking the dream

To awake in the morning with the day to myself
To recharge the batteries and think of my health
It all goes so quickly you have to be strong
Plan your escape, do not leave it too long

Time goes by at a terrible pace
You can be taken over as if running a race
But even racehorses have time for a graze
Take a grip of your life or it will end in a haze
I do not want much, I am not full of greed
But time to myself is a positive need

The Journey

The journey started some years ago
Paths have been trodden and seas crossed
Surroundings changed or rearranged
Emotions experienced and left their marks
Goals met, altered or adapted
Decisions at crossroads made
Mistakes overcome and priorities changed

Just going with the flow of traffic
Sometimes taking side tracks and pathways
Sometimes going with no destination in mind
Maps and guidebooks in their plenty
But only guides of what could be
Not what will be
Not how much further there is to go

Breakdowns along the way
Hold ups or just running out of fuel
This journey can take it out of you at times
Rests along the way are needed
Time for check-ups and MOTs of body and mind
Some U-turns allowed but never going back
Going on in whatever speed limit at the time
This journey will take as long as it will take

Body and Soul

If living and dying are part of the course
then the loss of a soul is a wasted resource
Are there so many that die every day
that non are recycled no one can say.

The body can rot and be manure for the ground
that keeps all life forms growing and the world going round
I cannot believe that to die is the end
just losing a body that no one can mend.

It is a wonderful feeling that there is somewhere to go
but no one can tell us so we go with the flow
If this experience called life to us is totally new
why the occasional feelings of déjà vu
Those feelings you get you cannot explain
maybe we just come back again and again.

Our Cosmos

I cannot begin to understand
The whole creation of our land
Of trees and oceans, plants and birds
Animals and humans in their herds
The planets, the universe and the stars
Other suns and moons not only ours
Black holes, the galaxy and space
The eternity of time to face
I hope this life is not only one
To drift through it all, could be fun

Walk not Run

Being alone in our own private space
Just another number in the human race
But why a race why not a stroll
Why strain the body, mind and soul

Do It

So there we are and off we go
A chance to live, a chance to grow
A chance to travel, see and learn
Things to enjoy, things to spurn
We stir our lives to fulfil our dreams
Some things for us, some not it seems
To open our sails, cast off and float
The winds of life will control our boat
Some cast off commitment and are free
For periods of their lives, to a varied degree
Thinking of doing loads of things
Or maybe some, but just in flings
However, whenever, work down the list
There is always cost and a bit of risk
Why say 'I wish' or 'if only' when
Others do it again and again
Priorities and circumstances can change
We have to adapt and re arrange
If the urge is strong and the mind is set
Go for your goals and avoid regret

The Jigsaw

Who knows how big the jigsaw will be
How hard it will be or how many pieces
How complicated, how much sea, sky or green
How much of the same to fill how big a space

We all hope for variety, those little pieces of colour
Some character, shapes and enjoyment
All these pieces we put in a box in the brain
Just a random collection especially when we are young

As we grow we tend to reflect, to survey the pieces
What have we done and how is the picture so far
We plan ahead to fill in gaps and fit in dreams
We plan the years ahead with ideas and hopefully time

Some are told of a terminal illness
Their time is short, the puzzle smaller
The pieces have to be put in order to make a picture
To come to terms with the ups and downs

Those special, valuable pieces will give the character
The background will reflect the major parts in your life
For those of us with time to add more pieces
Are we now content to sit back in a peaceful backdrop

This is coming to terms with our lot
To acknowledge our life, our achievements
You cannot change the pieces so highlight the good times
We all have large areas of the same it's how we colour them in.

Time & Life

Tick-tock goes the clock of time
The steady swing of the pendulum
The smooth motion of the cogs going round
The big clock face to keep us on track

Time has been ticking for many years
Every second of every day a new clock is formed
Every second of every day a clock dies
These are the hearts of babies, the hearts of the bereaved

Hearts tick-tock just like a clock
Valves pump the blood around the body
Blood takes the oxygen to every organ
The batteries we need are food and health
The pendulum is the body movements that keep us fit

In olden days clocks were repaired, now mainly replaced
In olden days heart failed and the body died
Now the hearts are repaired, new valves are fitted
Hearts can be replaced from donors not so lucky

The tick-tock of time does not end when a clock is broken
The tick-tock of life does not end when a heart is broken

The Family Bond

You are born with two parents in the natural way
a bond that progresses day after day
They guide you and protect you while you mature
into your own personality to decide what life is for

When you leave home you still need them there
because when you need help you know that they care
The visits and help you tend to neglect
they will always be there that is what you expect

But taking for granted the things that you need
while rushing around and trying to succeed
Then you are hit by the news of a loss
one parent dies and the message comes across
The bond that was there has now taken a change
there is only one parent to take up the reins

They are now stricken by being alone
they have to work hard at retaining the home
The one that you have lost and expected to last
at an age when their friendship was still in your grasp

The feeling of not seeing them as much as you could
can fill you with guilt but will not do any good
The one that is left is still there for you
they now need your friendship and you need them too

I know it is nature to lose family and friends
do not let arguments linger you must make amends
We must stay together for ourselves and the dead
the family bond becomes a friendship instead

We all grow stubborn and do not want to be told
we get fixed in our ways as we get old
But when people advise us it is for the reason they care
so keep helping our loved ones in this bondship we share

The Spider

There is a large brown spider who lives inside my home
Whenever I decide to relax he then decides to roam

He runs around the carpet and all around the chairs
The fact that I am in there he never really cares

I have not found his spider's web, I have not cleaned of late
I do not mind his presence, he has become a mate

He never really bothers me, he never comes near my seat
I only hope that one day he does not get under my feet

'If'

If I was you and you were me
where in this life would we be

Would it be just the same
You and me in a different game

Would we have met along the way
Maybe yes maybe no who can say

The Age Attitude

Of all the things I have wanted to do
most have been done except a few.
The things that are left can be done in due course
a goal left to go for when I have the resource.
Things have before been done on the cheap
but as you get older the risks are more deep.

When you are young there is time to regain
mid-life is different, a secure future your aim.
For when you are old why not be content
instead of living off the cheque the social have sent.

Pen to Paper

Ideas to write going around in my head
that takes up my time, chores should be done instead.
What is this urge to get it on paper
The clock ticks on, it is later and later.
Maybe just doing it will get my thoughts through
Will they ever be published I do not have a clue.

Role Reversal

Mother was at home
To feed and care for us boys
To feed and care for grandma
To do the books for father's business

She was secretary to the local builder
Then secretary at the local primary school
Her boys were old enough by then
She had steered us through adolescence

We boys went off to college
Grandma lived on
But father died early
The routine had changed

Grandma went into a home
Mother moved from village to town
The WI and British Legion took over
From Secretary to Treasurer to Chair

Mother could not be idle
She kept busy and active
Keeping a home for us boys
Keeping alive family links

Mother turned 80 with a family lunch
Grandma had died
The WI and British legion kept her busy
But change was on the way

The mind became tired
The body slowed down
The busy life diminished
Mother was changing

The changes got worse
Coping with it all got harder
Mother was becoming a dependant
She was no longer her old self

Us boys took the roles as parents
Mother became our charge
We were reversing the roles
Life changing for all of us

From retirement home to nursing home
From strong and confident to dependent
From alert to confused
From the Queen to the Pawn

Mother had become a child
Us boys watched mother disappear
We watched the quality of life fade
We watched her slip away

Mother even at the end filled a space
She was our mother
She had got us were we are today
We had a parent

Now we are the elders
We will slow down
We will follow the trials of old age
We will do it as best as fate allows

Man's Best Friends

Doggie housemates are the best
They love their walks and then they rest
Their special welcome when you get home
With doggies around you are never alone

Doggie Habits

Doggies do what doggies do
They bark or yap, they pee and pooh
The barks and pees are fully allowed
But pick up the pooh because they have fouled

To foul the places people go
Definitely not: the signs say so
Way out in the country we pretend to forget
Just part of nature, no one to upset

Being Aware

I think of religions, their paths and belief
Their harsh regimes and sins they relieve
I choose not one but pick and mix
Worldly troubles they cause but cannot fix

I believe in science for the beginning of time
The rising of empires that grow then decline
The make up of plants, animals and man
Abusing our planet being the biggest sham

I want to think we are not alone
An enormous universe there to roam
Stars that shine and planets out of reach
Facts our planet and galaxy still have to teach

I love to watch, to sit and be aware
To watch the world in silence but trying not to stare
Not to stare at people but to guess what they do
What lives they live, where and with who

The whole of nature busy to survive
A constant battle to live and stay alive
Seasons wet, cold, windy but also sunny days
Sunrises and sunsets to set the skies ablaze

People get ill and I have seen them die
The moment they go you feel their energy fly
Energy gone they are now but a shell
Gone where who can tell

News around the world travels as the media grows
Nothing is kept quiet, everyone knows
The urge to travel becomes more of a worry
Plan it well, do not be in a hurry

Not going along the easy route
During rush hour when people shout and hoot
Pick your time to suit your needs
If it is only a dream then plant the seeds

My surroundings, my universe and my life
My achievements, my journey, my strife
For when I lay down to let the energy expire
My universe will end, all that I am will retire

An Age Thing

Less years ahead less time for fun
The choice to walk and not to run
Too late to alter and change my ways
Just doing things to fill my days

Alone

I'd like to write of love, companionship and fun
I'd like to say how fortunate are some
I have had partners but at the wrong time
If they had come along now then that would be fine

Now that I have lost them I can only compare
Now that I am ready nobody is there
I have not given up nor full of remorse
Just going about things, letting life take its course

You get used to doing things and coping alone
This is purely a thought, not meant as a moan

Mental Blank

I had a thought the other day
A thought that came then went away
A thought my mind will not replay
What it was I cannot say

Until my Rest

We must be here to do certain things
To see what every daybreak brings
To fill the time and do our best
Until we die and take our rest

Just Different

Do not always do what others do
For I am me and you are you
Somethings may mirror an other's feat
Just being different not always unique

Days Alive

I have been alive for over twenty-two-thousand days
I recall a very small proportion of these
They are all stored somewhere in my brain
People and events will trigger off recollections
Highlights will always stay in the conscious
Others will drift from conscious to subconscious

What I did last week, last month or last year
These can be lost in the short-term memory
Memories are memories but not always date stamped
I can remember doing this or that but when
What day of the month or even what year
Was it morning, noon or night

Computers have memory sticks and hard drives
Our hard drives are called the brain
We just need memory sticks to access the file
We are sophisticated computers
We need rebooting now and then
We have an endless storage capacity

No printer so no hard copies of the files within
Word and mouth the only way to forward contents
Many events we have shared with others
Our memory files may have the same title
The contents of the file will never be duplicated

Our computer will crash the day we die
No second hand ones are available
Brain transplants are not yet available
The refresh button no longer works
One body, one brain, one life

This Moment in Time

Ifs and buts are not for me
No crystal ball to gaze and see
Where we is, is where we are at
Today is now and no going back

The Post

In the morning the post arrives
The contents often affect our lives
The bills and bad news cloud our day
The nice things make us smile and say
Things are not so bad just for a bit
Those paper packages with stamps stuck on by spit

Why

We are born to live and then to die
Don't ask me how, when or why

World AIDS Day Candlelit Vigil

For this candlelit vigil the reason we are here
To remember those we have lost who were precious and dear

The virus that got them is a cruel act of fate
That sweeps through the community at an alarming rate

Now we have drugs that will extend our years
Although the longer you are on them you still have the fears

Some we have lost did not have that choice
To drop a few pills, prolong their lives and still have a voice

We look around the room and see sadness and regret
Of losing our loved ones who we can never forget

Each of the candles is a friend who has died
Their souls are now free, we have grieved and we have cried

This dance of the candles that just sparkle and shine
A happy thought that through it all and whenever one will be mine

For in the midst of the sadness you will dance and will glitter
All the pain and worry gone so be at peace with that thought and do
not feel bitter

We all have to die it's the quality of life we must sustain
So go on with whatever, smile when you can and see you again

Just Weary

No expectations, no long-term goals or ambitions
Just using what has been learnt along the way
Whatever the body will allow
Living with the hand life has dealt you

Forget the what could have beens
No expectations so no disappointments
No future plans or comparisons
Just going day by day, month by month

Void of any enthusiasm or energy
The mind and the body are weary
Too restless to relax or unwind
Things to be done bills to pay

Peace and contentment your main desire
Maybe some day maybe not
Maybe a new card game, new cards
New dice or new players around the table

Maybe, maybe is what will keep you going
Maybe has to be better than never
Positive thoughts and good health
These are the plus points to remember

My Seasons

I am the centre of my world,
I have my seasons my nights and days
My dull, dreary and drizzly days, my beautiful sunny days
Fabulous sunsets and rainbows,
Those crisp and clear frosty landscapes

The thunder and lightning, the dramatic floods
The winds of change to clear my path, to blow away those
problem dead leaves that have fallen from the glorious deciduous
trees in you, autumn, ready for the crispness of winter.
The old friends and memories in your head are like bulbs that
hide away and then burst into bloom, back into your life
to say spring is here, get ready for summer and fun

To be in my world you need to be prepared for all the seasons
forever changing, never knowing what to wear or how to protect
yourself from the elements, there is fate, there is freedom,
there is fresh air and time for a walk.

A Helping Hand

This thing called life has been around a long time
there is love, lust and greed and even more crime

The way that you grow up and the support that you need
has not been the same for us all it must be agreed

In nature the animals and plants that are strong
get on with the process without making a song

But the human race has been encouraged to share
to pick up the weak and our time we must share

You do not always get thanks for your time and your tasks
it may make you feel good if somebody asks

Those that are helpless and need all the help they can get
this must be done without any regret

Some are just takers and will not help themselves
they believe life has dumped them and are left on the shelves

We all have our problems and must do what we can
there may be a time in your life that reverses the plan

Living and Dying

Some people are eager to know what happens at the end
but everyone knows you cannot see round a bend

Why be in such a hurry to finish the story
it may be quite nice but could also be gory

Try living each moment however many the days
the end may be close or a long time away

I cannot deny that the occasional thought
can fill you with wonder or make you quite fraught

As long as time, whenever it started,
there have been thousands of people all now departed

If all the things that have died were still lying around
the world would be full with no place on the ground

What really happens when the life bell rings
you know bloody well that another begins

The Alarm Clock

I am breathing in oxygen
I am setting my alarm for eight
I do this nearly every day
I brush my teeth and take my tablets
Shave every other day
Days at work are less than before
There are household chores to do
There is the garden to tend

Going out and meeting friends
This has taken a decline of late
Books replace crap TV and adverts
Illness of family and friends become the norm
The clock is still ticking
Big hand passing over little hand
Pages of the calendar are turned

This is where I am today
In fact it is where I've been for a while
I should break away and be creative
Throw caution to the wind
But I do not
I set my alarm for eight
Then go to bed

I am not sad or depressed

I have done many things
Done a fair bit of travelling
Have and have had many good friends
But where to go next
How much do I want to move on
Have I created my own private cocoon

The same routine with the alarm for eight
Just killing time for whatever or whenever
Maybe I am waiting for a sign
Maybe a revolutionary event will occur
A burst of happiness and laughter
Something to kick start the old have-a-go instinct
There will be a sequel to this, there has to be!

Me

I am what I am
Things are as they are
You do what you can
And just reach for a star

Life

Learning while living is a natural thing
You die at the end just like you begin

Three Score Years

Three score years and ten
Three score years and then
Sign off or do it again

The Phone Thing

There are phones in your home your office and paybox
when you make a phone call you know what it costs
now there are mobiles and a hell of a range
that eat up your notes instead of your change

You remember a number that you knew of from old
and then find out that they have altered the code
to ring a company and ask a small question
means you have to be patient and hear the selection

This constant connection at the end of a phone
I suppose there is the feeling of not being alone
the one thing I love is my answering device
you can screen all the calls and pick out the nice
of having the chance to talk when you like
makes time to yourself our personal right

One of Life's Black Holes

Being stripped of my armour, my security, my position and my identity in this world, I am at this moment in time, jobless.

Now, naked and vulnerable, bare to face the harsh elements of life, bills to be paid, food to eat, to try to maintain some kind of self-esteem, a position in this life that is essential to hang on to and to be preserved at all times.
I do not delude myself of being on any kind of pedestal, just to have a comfortable enough life with my own shell in which to hide away, full of my own belongings to create a personality space and creature comforts; as long as the mortgage payments are met.

The longer the feeling of nakedness then the less you venture out, away from the shell of comfort and for shorter spells at a time.
Often returning to your foetal state, staying curled up in bed, your substitute womb, safe and warm where you can drift off into a cosy slumber, a void to pretend for a while that the rest of the world does not exist, the harsh elements of life are no longer there as long as you stay curled up under the duvet.

But hey wake up this is not OK, we were ejected from our mother's womb to get on with things, we do not know exactly what things but must make an effort and survive.

We have many choices to be made, a multitude of paths that could be taken and mistakes to overcome, we are alone, we no longer have an umbilical cord to rely on, but this can and must be done as it has been done for thousands of years before us.

The truth is that you are not what you do for a living but what living you do and with a certain amount of luck, good fortune, the right guidance and reasonable health the process might even have its moments and at times be quite enjoyable.

What Is

The expected life span of whatever is
The pitfalls, accidents and dangers are
Predictions are only predictions
The past is just the past
The present the present and the future
another assumption or prediction or
just a reason to live out the cycle
for whatever reason that is

Life

A life time, to live and breathe
A life to live through every need
The ups and downs we will succeed
This pre-planned course we must believe

We must believe in ourselves for a reason
The cold and warmth of every season
The acts of friendship and of treason
Our bodies and souls in perfect adhesion

Plans and Diversions

Happy days of childhood, school and college, days of what will be

What we will be doing in five or ten years' time, setting goals and

dreams

Of paths to be trodden and diversions we may take along the way

Changing course as circumstances and opportunities arise

Hopefully fulfilling some of those early quests we made

But also doing and achieving much more along the way

When all is said and done have the unplanned parts of life

compensated for the plans left undone

There comes a stage when you say enough, slow down

Time to reflect, to appreciate all of your yesterdays and to enjoy today

Slow down with plans for tomorrow for now goals can be more

flexible.

It is often the journey to achieve the goal that is the thrill

Once you have reached it you will just have to think of another

Playing, Bluffing or Both

Getting through this life is like a game of poker, first you need to learn about the cards in the pack and the basic rules of how to play. You are then dealt the hand but it is how good you are at playing it, do you play it safe all the time, part of the time or bluff your way throughout the game

Playing safe is good, keeping a certain amount of control but you can miss out on opportunities along the way so a few gambles and a bit of bluffing is good. It may or may not come up trumps but it is worth a try occasionally to keep the game interesting especially as you become more confident and learn how to read the other players around the table.

When you are lucky enough to get a great hand then this is one of life's bonuses, the mistake is to say yippee my luck has changed I must gamble more. Luck is luck and must not be taken for granted, accept it as a gift of life they can come in runs or only occasionally. You cannot create luck, you can only play or bluff, even bluffing takes skill to be successful and can be quite costly if you get it wrong

The Barter in Life

Repay good deeds not necessarily to the same person but
to someone along the way.
Learn from people, then apply it to your own life or to
help someone else.
Never be too busy to help if you can, prioritise because you will only
feel bad if you do not help and cannot expect others to be available
when you may need them. Go out of your way occasionally and the
rewards can be great, maybe not at the time but later in your life.
If you suffer with people you will learn through them to suffer
yourself. Strength can come in the form of a few words said to you
at a bus stop that make you smile, remember those words and repeat
them to encourage someone else to do the same.
When not feeling well and not able to give is the time when the barter
comes in and something good is done for you.
We are not angels, we do not always know what to do, sometimes we
do it wrong but we try and we learn so the rights can correct
the wrongs.

The Grey Times

The light fades somewhere between a full day and a quiet evening
A halfway time of day, a halfway mood that seems to last for ever
The days are not so full just a treadmill of chores that suffocate time
Time that was once for fun, gaiety and contentment

The evenings quiet but not relaxing void of comfort and affection
This halfway state has frozen the clock and the calendar
The seasons seem to have no effect not even on the weather
A cloudy head numbs all reaction to our surroundings

Those exhilarating early dawns of a new day seem to be wasted
Wasted on contemplation of getting through another day
Not just today but the weeks and months ahead
This constant treadmill that appears to lead to eternity

Sure there are positive thoughts of what could be nice
What we think would bring back that smile of contentment
But we are weary, addicted to our own numbness
Hard to shake off that feeling of 'this is my lot'

This halfway state of mind, this halfway time of day
Memories become cloudy, the contacts you have are spaced
further away

Energy to do what was fun and effortless now on low batteries

But where is the charger or supply of new batteries

We strive on in a vain hope that repair is possible

That our charger or battery replacements will be found

To reset this body and mind and rewind the clock

To pass through the night towards a bright new dawn

The Body Needs

Clothes to keep us warm
Shelter to keep us dry and safe
Food to keep the engine working
Sex to fulfil the body's needs
Medicines to keep us healthy and
free from pain
Money to pay for the above
But
when you die you drop your body
what a great idea

Drifting off

Lying in bed with your eyes closed
The clock hardly moves so you have not even dozed

Lying awake and trying to sleep
Only a little will do, not necessarily deep

Just thinking of something to make you drift off
Then just as you do you awake with a cough

Get up for a while and watch the TV
In your favourite armchair with a nice cup of tea

Maybe the body clock has got all confused
Whatever the reason you are not amused

You take it for granted this sleeping at night
And most of the time you do it all right

But resting the body at the end of the day
Must be done after working and after play

Just relax as you can and try to switch off your mind
It will happen quite naturally as you unwind

Your body knows well what it must do
It's a wonderful thing and it's there just for you

Motorway Driving

While driving along the motorway without any sights
Except an ocean of darkness and some flickering lights

From one place to the next is your reason and intention
Then your mind starts to wander and there's a short intervention

What if you follow the cat's eyes and drive on instead
Your mind and accelerator keep pushing ahead

There are times in your life when you're free with no plan
It is then that you must do it for the reason you can

It can be a complete waste of petrol and also of time
But to go on with a whim is a feeling sublime

It is the feeling of doing it just for the fact
That if nothing comes of it you can always retract

If you occasionally try and not do the norm
You will enjoy the drive through moonshine or storm

But as you get tired the fantasy is often less clear
So you come to your exit and change down a gear

Hangover and Stress Relief

The morning after the night before when your head and stomach are aching, when your body is suffering from being filled with something it does not want, your recovery will be long and slow. To speed up the process put your fingers down your throat and eject the unwanted contents, your body and head will thank you for it and recovery will be less uncomfortable.

Likewise when your body and head are full of pain as a result of anxiety and stress, often caused by other people, the symptoms are the same as a hangover. You have let things swell up inside, things that are not welcome and must be ejected as above. Open your mouth and let rip, offload, write it down, clear the air but do something. Things will not go away but you will not have them burning up in the body and head to the same extent.

Communication

Communication was easy when we were all around
just like the animals that stay in a crowd
But we started to wander and moving away
contact was not so easy day after day

Then came the letter that had to be stamped
Today a system that has not been revamped
Later the telephone connected by cable
communicating wherever, not needing a table

For those not comfortable with writing this made them relax
although now you can do it by sending a fax
With all this technology you can keep up with the set
especially now if you're part of the net

The world can converse with no need to travel
while businesses connect, friends and family babble
This world wide community just coming and going
but basic contact is physical and our numbers are growing

Although this is changing and you do not need to meet
a partner can be found it is very discreet
Community life is now purely by choice
you can do it all on your own by computers or voice

Are things now improving or have they got worse
decide for yourself be it a blessing or curse

Boris

Boris oh Boris my four-legged friend
16 years of companionship from beginning to end

I found him in a market abandoned and tied to a tree
I knew straight away that this dog was for me

He was an Aussie and I was a Pom.
So I brought him back home to the land I was from

A true bond of friendship that no one could break
The welcome, the walks you could not recreate

Our lives with each other was never a tie
But life spans are different and pets often die

The death of a friend is a terrible revelation
I decided to go for a pet cremation

What to do with the ashes was a bit of a thought
Some wide open space we both knew was at Ashton Court

Along with fellow dog lover we let the ashes ascend
Back to nature they went and goodbye to a friend

Memory

There are now so many things in my head
One can only assume they will be there until I am dead
Then when I die the hard drive will be gone
But if the soul has a floppy it may well carry on

Must Do

Must do this and must do that
Can often be a load of crap
To breathe and eat as animals do
Are the basic needs for me and you

Compromise

You will never see and do it all
The world is big and our life time small
Enjoy the paths that are for you
Plan your time and think it through

Not All There

There are times that I do not feel totally complete, being with people
and doing things but not really all there
The mind and body seem to be in a transient state, the mouth is
conversing but the mind is not really all there
Going through social acts and being part of the crowd yet with a
physical and mental void, not really all there
A partial out of body experience, a bit of a zombie, a wondering mind,
being there but not totally all there
If the mind is drifting then it is not telling me where, no explanation
or reason for not being totally all there

Born on Earth

Everything that is born on this earth dies on this earth,
plants, birds, insects, animals and people however big or small.

Some insects, butterflies and plants have a very small life span
unlike trees that can live for centuries.
This is the truth, a fact, life then death

It is the way that you die that is the thing to worry about
maybe long and drawn out with lots of suffering
maybe when the body is tired and can take no more
when the face becomes relaxed and we are at peace

Could this world be like a womb from which we emerge
To continue into the vast array of planets and stars, who knows
Worry not, it will happen one way or the other,
we will not be the first to find out or the last.

Life throws at you what you have to take.
Do not take the easy way out, it will only upset family and friends
Take the easy way and you will just be sent back to do it again.
Be strong and survive the ups and the downs for they are your test,
your exam to pass or fail.

Holiday Package Deal on Earth

Get born as a human and get your arse slapped then cry
Go through all the ups and downs of childhood
Make loads of decisions some good some bad
Work hard to pay for clothing, food and shelter
Retire as early as possible, if you make it that long
Maybe get ill or just grow old and die

Maybe you get killed on the way
Length of holiday unknown and it is free of charge
Attractions depend on your luck and your attitude
There is no travel insurance, no guarantees
No refunds the only concession is
If you get it wrong you may get a return flight
Bon Voyage

Our Living Space

Blossom and bloom in your surroundings, wilt a bit in the sun and drink in the rain, people watch, listen to the sounds around, smile or frown for like art it does not have to be liked it is there to create an effect. Personalities are the likes and dislikes, opinions and what you do with your life.

The space and things around you very much affect your moods and energy, be it at work, home or the times in between. Surroundings are places, people, buildings, your home, pictures, plants or animals, these are the material things.

A beautiful view on a sunny day, a rainbow, the natural things that can lift you as much as, if not more than, people. Too much emphasis is often put on people, they are just part of it all, they only fill certain spaces as much as trees, mountains and oceans.

Be open to all around you, absorb nature, watch and listen to the birds sing, the sound of the tide on a pebble beach, relax and be part of it all because you are the traveller the observer but to others you are part of their surroundings.

If you have barren thoughts and wait for others to come along and plant shrubs and flowers in your mind without doing some work yourself then beware, the weeds of life may take over. Religion, cults and dominant people prey on barren thoughts they move in and plant their own seeds and you are then part of someone else's garden.

The effort will be rewarded by living in an original and rewarding space, your space that hopefully people will enjoy visiting and will be happy to be around. They may at times be envious but that will often trigger them off to say I must do something like that myself. Learn from others who you respect or are envious of for that is part of it, the living, learning and growing in wisdom and strength. Learn from the people of the past their books and thoughts that are still alive while they themselves are dead.

Finance and cost are not important as seeds of life, cuttings from friends will bloom the same as expensive plants from a garden centre, they may take a bit longer to thrive but will mean more every year they grow and will be a stronger part of you.

Remember that nature has been around long before us all, it will still be there hopefully live years ahead of us. The wonders of the world, the breath-taking scenery, the red sky at night, the thunder and lightning will just carry on and the fact that you and I are no longer will have no effect on them at all, they are there for us not us for them.

Our planet and home is forever changing through hurricanes, earthquakes, drought and floods, it has for centuries from before the ice age and beyond. We cause our own world-wide disasters like wars and global warming but cannot repair the damage, that is left to nature, that great and wonderful power that is there to cover up our mistakes and make its own changes along the way.

Plants, animals and insects adapt as their surroundings change, resistance to drugs and pesticides that once would have destroyed. We are only animals of a sort but are stubborn and expect to stay the same so try changing the surroundings to have our own way. An arrogant thought and a thankless task to think that although we have evolved like the rest that we are now the masters of it all.

Play on if that is the game and path you have chosen, but do not play only to win, I put my money on nature every time.

The Filing Cabinet ofLife

The people you meet along this path of life must be assessed for how they are to you, they must be put into your filing cabinet of life some of them will fit into one file only while others can go into many files. Some files will be large but on the whole the very special files will be quality not quantity.

You have to go through the people disappointment process to learn to do the filing effectively, to say I like that person for this or that reason but ! the but is the file they will not be in.

That does not mean that they never will, people change they can come out of one file just as easily as they can go into others, keep those files up to date to reduce stress and disappointment.

THE FILES

Friends

These are mainly your Christmas card list, those you know and have known that you like and do not want to lose touch with. They are often in other files or have been in the past and if you meet up again will return to the closer and every day files.

Time, distance and circumstances can keep us apart but true friendship never dies, they stay in that file even after death because they had an effect on your life and are still a part of it.

Family

A group of people around you in your early years, when you start life and start to develop into an individual. At this stage start filing them as soon as you can for they must be assessed by the same rules as everyone else.

The ones you keep in touch with will thank you for it because you are doing it for the right reason. Never take anyone for granted it is not fair on you or on them.

Fun

Great fun to be with and have a laugh but no real part in your life, call them the medicine, the pick me ups of life. There are naturally many who are in other files, who are a lot more than just fun.

Trust

This is the one to watch, the one that can change very quickly, you may well have thought you could but you cannot, the reverse can always be true which is great but do some re-filing immediately.

Affection

This comes in many forms, can be long term or a brief encounter but they have all had a strong effect on your life a valuable file as all the names are very special people to you.

Work

Work mates can make or break your working life, a large chunk of your life, they are very often people who fit into other files, sometimes just for that employment and often on a more permanent basis.

Support and Dependability

Very special people, you may not have that many in this file if you have been honest with yourself, this is true bonding, to feel relaxed and open with this person. To be able to discuss whatever, to value their opinion and to be there when you need them. Most of these people will be in other files, cherish them and be honoured to have their names in your file.

Respect

This can contain names of those you do not know personally but they have an effect on your life like role models. They will be names in other files, some good files and some not so good, you do not have to like someone to respect them.

Distrust

If you put names in this file then remember why, remember they are in here you can still like someone even if you do not trust them.

Unreliable

There are those who are just not reliable, it is often because they try to take on too much not always because they do not care. Do not disregard them they often have other qualities and often mean well it is just the way they are.

Tolerable

Nice is all you can say about them, not an important file, just somewhere to put these people you meet along the way.

Intolerable

Do not waste time on this file it will just make you feel better putting those people in it.

Press Pause

Stop the clock, put everything on hold, I need time to catch up, there is so much left undone, so much to do now and in the near future, in the short term is bad enough but to think of the long term, what a nightmare.

It is not that all these tasks are necessarily difficult, some can be done quite easily and quickly, it is just the time and energy to do them that is the problem. After all you have to be in the mood for certain chores let alone making time to relax, unwind and switch off for a while.

Very often, you think you are winning, getting on top of it all, then more tasks appear, some new and some that have been created by old ones that have still to be tackled.

The head in the sand is a lovely idea in theory but in practice they are still there when you surface, often worse than before. A stitch in time they say but it is the time that is the problem not the stitch, although a simple stitch can be a pain if you do not have the right needle or thread. Then you have to go and buy them once you have found a shop that sells what you want and often have to buy a whole packet when you only need one.

Some days you get up in the perfect mood and tick off one job after another a great day when it happens, but then you can waste the whole day doing a simple task that keeps going wrong, usually when you try to do something when you are tired or not in the mood.

There are no rewind or fast forward buttons so you have to be strong minded and press the pause button, take some time to yourself and say I am not available I have things to do, then get on and do as many as possible in that time.

A stop button would not work, it would have the same effect as the head in the sand so pressing the restart button would become harder and harder as time went on.

The pause button is the one to press and press again, get used to using it when things get on top of you so that you can catch up and clear yourself some space and time for a while until the next load comes along and it will as sure as night follows day!

Deliverance Please

Pompous thoughts and greed of this human race
As we become more and more of a total disgrace
Purely animals of a kind to stroll the world
With twisted attitudes to kill and fight as bombs are hurled

Basic animal behaviour is to kill only to eat
Not this strange feeling that we are the elite
Killing and torturing or just to maim
Even our own breed, this must be insane

The way people look or what religion they follow
These acts of indifference and cruelty are hard to swallow
Natural disasters and diseases are nature's way of control
Not allowing injustices then giving parole

Man has an urge to have, not live and let live
Ethnic cleansing and other horrors, we should never forgive
But with mixed marriages now happening in every nation
Adapting nature towards the future of a brand new creation

Grass being greener on the other side
The lawn may be better but easier for weeds to hide
If only cultures could be left on their own
Without foreign intervention, trying to change them and moan

See and hear what others around the world have to suffer

Just growing up in this age gets sadder, harder and tougher

Human rights are forever falling as dictators ascend

It is not only us, but our survival and nature they offend

Is there an end, answer, or do we just do what we can

Maybe total self-destruction is part of the plan

No justification for the suffering, the wasting of lives

For as quickly as they are murdered another arrives

The People Plants

The variety of trees, the oaks and willows of varied strength that grow stronger and stronger as they mature and survive.

The weeds that are everywhere and will strangle other plants just to survive, the ethnic cleansing.

The flowers that bloom to reproduce unless cut down to rot in a vase or to be eaten, the accidents in life. Even the young buds, the children are not safe, they can be killed or maimed before they have a chance to grow.

Deforestation a form of ethnic cleansing or wars, not for food or even for the wood just that they dare to be where others want to be, selfishness, greed, politics or religion all have their own pompous justifications.

There are plenty of weed killers, some temporary some systemic, but they kill and pollute like wars, bombs, gases and nuclear warfare. They pollute what is left, what the original occupiers were killed for, which means that they are worse off than they were in the first place, they have polluted their own space.

We all have our roots, our upbringing, which will determine how we grow, we put out our leaves and branches to test the space around and hope that it is safe to blossom and grow.

The seed and planting is a major key, some are lucky, some find it hard and some are transplanted not always successfully, some wither and die unable to readjust or because of the way in which they were uprooted in the first place.

The seeds from plants can live dormant for years and years and for this reason were here before us and will probably survive long after us, only nature and the universe will decide when enough is enough, natural disasters cannot be controlled, those that are will only create bigger effects on the planet in the future.

People in green houses should not throw stones, we have created our own greenhouse but we are still throwing stones.

Those Drowning Periods

I used to love life now I just live it

Sometimes loneliness and depression causes you to switch off into a
ghost-like attitude, you float among those that are living their lives
but you are not part of it.

A bit of mindless fun would be nice, someone to hug and to share
things with would be fantastic.

There can be a strong feeling of déjà vu, of having done most things
at some time or another and now have no interest in planning ahead
just filling up time until the next stage whatever that is.

You have to get through this life that has been given to you one way
or the other and then reach the natural end.

I am not worried or scared nor am I in any hurry but am ready and
willing

Just make it as peaceful and as painless as possible.

People on a Plate

A relationship is like a well-balanced meal
For the carnivore who likes their meat tasty and lean
or the vegetarian who prefers other proteins, the substitutes
these are the main decisions for the meal but what to serve with it.

Imagine that your partner or prospective partner is the main course
on first impressions a tasty bit of meat to sink your teeth into
just the flavour you are in the mood for.
So you go for it but there is still the rest of the plate to fill.

The vegetable will be the personality, things you have in common,
the carbohydrates the substance the comfort and filling that will keep
you going and keep hunger at bay.
Take care as too much red meat can cause heart failure as can
overeating and the wrong diet.